IMAGES
of America

SAGUARO
NATIONAL PARK

Pictured is 1940s signage describing Saguaro National Park. (Courtesy of Western Archeological Conservation Center.)

Welcome to Saguaro National Park. (Courtesy Western Archeological Conservation Center.)

ON THE COVER: Saguaro National Park aid Dee Dodge is teaching Tucson Girl Scouts about desert life. (Courtesy Western Archeological Conservation Center.)

IMAGES
of America

SAGUARO
NATIONAL PARK

Jane Eppinga

ARCADIA
PUBLISHING

Published by Arcadia Publishing
Charleston, South Carolina

Printed in the United States of America

Library of Congress Control Number: 2012937628

For all general information, please contact Arcadia Publishing:
Telephone 843-853-2070
Fax 843-853-0044
E-mail sales@arcadiapublishing.com
For customer service and orders:
Toll-Free 1-888-313-2665

Visit us on the Internet at www.arcadiapublishing.com

To all who make the wonders of the national parks available to the world

CONTENTS

Acknowledgments   6

Introduction   7

1.   The Park and Politics   9

2.   Critters and Cactus Views   21

3.   Those Who Came Before   33

4.   Ranchers and Miners   45

5.   Stewards of the Park   63

6.   The People and the Park   89

Bibliography   126

Index   127

ACKNOWLEDGMENTS

A book is never entirely the work of one person, and so it is the case with *Saguaro National Park*. This is the time to round up the usual individuals and organizations and recognize them for their generous assistance: the Arizona Historical Society Library and the Library of Congress; June Gallegos, Denver Regional Office of the National Park Service; Andy Fisher, Vicki Powers, and Ronald Beckwith, Saguaro National Park; Khaleel Saba, Western Archeological Conservation Center (WACC); Wendy Davis, Department of Agriculture, University of Arizona, Tucson; Richard Egner, Harper's Ferry; Robert Arnberger, William Paleck, Doug Morris, Franklin Parker, and Sarah Craighead, former superintendents of Saguaro National Park; Lynda Sánchez, images of Joe Carithers; the William J. Clinton Presidential Library; the Franklin D. Roosevelt Library; and Janelle Weakly, Arizona State Museum. Alene Fletcher and Betty Cook helped me locate pioneer graves. No book sees the light of day without a publisher and an editor such as Arcadia and Stacia Bannerman, Kristie Kelly, and the Arcadia staff. Finally, the biggest contributors are those pioneers who left their stories and marks on a place called Saguaro National Park.

INTRODUCTION

As of 2012, the United States has more than 50 protected national parks, which are operated by the National Park Service (NPS). National monuments may be established by the president, but national parks must be established by an act of the US Congress. The Organic Act of 1916 created the NPS "to conserve the scenery and the natural and historic objects and wildlife therein and to provide for the enjoyment of the same in such manner and by such means as will leave them unimpaired for the enjoyment of future generations." The US National Park System consists of hundreds of parks, monuments, and historical sites spread across 49 states and the territories of American Samoa and the US Virgin Islands. Each one offers a glimpse into the natural beauty and history of America. National parks are protected by the American Antiquities Act of 1906, which reads in part:

> Be it enacted by the Senate and House of Representatives of the United States of America in Congress assembled, That any person who shall appropriate, excavate, injure, or destroy any historic or prehistoric ruin or monument, or any object of antiquity, situated on lands owned or controlled by the Government of the United States, without the permission of the Secretary of the Department of the Government having jurisdiction over the lands on which said antiquities are situated, shall, upon conviction, be fined in a sum of not more than five hundred dollars or be imprisoned for a period of not more than ninety days, or shall suffer both fine and imprisonment, in the discretion of the court.

Long before Pres. Herbert Hoover and his executive proclamation made Saguaro a national monument on March 1, 1933, there was the land with its magnificent saguaro cacti. The region was inhabited by prehistoric indigenous people who lived off the plants of the desert. It is one thing to declare a national park or monument on paper, but it is quite another to institute it. The road toward becoming Saguaro National Park would be long and tortuous. In 1891, the national government set aside forestland on the public domain as National Forest Reserves. By assuming the role of perpetual owner and administrator of these lands and their resources, the government began the reversal of land privatization on the frontier. The forest service allotted grazing rights to the ranchers. After 13 weeks under forest service administration, Pres. Franklin D. Roosevelt transferred Saguaro and 15 other monuments to the National Park Service. The park service did not want six of the monuments, including Saguaro. The decision, however, lay with Secretary of the Interior Harold Ickes, who was persuaded to keep it. Local rancher James Converse ran 100 or more head of cattle on the land. The state and university charged him 3¢ per acre to lease land with no restriction on the number of livestock that could be grazed. Ickes insisted that all valid rights would be respected. Determined that Saguaro National Monument would be administered by the park service, NPS assistant director Arno Cammerer proposed to use the area as a research reserve.

When the National Park Service asked the University of Arizona to donate its part of this land to the federal government, Dr. Homer Shantz, president of the university, asked for $56,000 as reimbursement. By July 1936, after John Harrison obtained options from all the private landowners, he met with Frank Pinkley, who favored returning land to the forest service, with the park service getting title to the cactus area. Harrison contacted Rep. Isabella Greenway and Sen. Carl Hayden regarding the plan, stating that it had the support of Frank Pinkley. Arizona governor B.B. Moeur contacted Secretary of the Interior Ickes to request an emergency fund to purchase the state and private land within the monument boundary. From 1936 through 1939, drought conditions prevailed throughout southern Arizona. Several changes in ownership had occurred starting in 1939, and in 1943, the Happy Valley Allotment became active.

The Pantano Allotment passed to Allison Armour in 1939, and Armour sold his allotment to Helen Lichtenstein in 1941. During that year, Robert Chatfield-Taylor purchased the Rukin Jelks property and obtained the Rincon Allotment with it. These land sales prompted a new policy that each time a ranch changed ownership, a slight reduction would be made in the number of stock permitted to graze on the allotment. This occurred for the first time in 1945, when Eduardo Carrillo's widow sold the ranch to Joe Lewis Hartzell and the grazing allotment was reduced by 10 percent.

Several ranches exchanged hands in the 1950s. Converse sold his Tanque Verde Ranch to Kenneth Kaecker. The ranch controlling the Pantano Allotment passed through several owners, including Bill Veeck of baseball fame. On August 25, 1959, Assistant Secretary of the Interior Roger Ernst issued Public Land Order 1963, which would restored 7,600 acres of the Tucson Mountain Park west of Tucson to mining. This action caused an intense protest and forced Ernst to suspend the effective restoration date. In 1960, Rep. Stewart Udall introduced a bill by which federal land leased to Pima County for the park would be transferred to Saguaro National Monument. Subsequently, Rep. Morris K. Udall, who replaced his brother Stewart Udall when the latter became Secretary of the Interior, initiated a bill to have 15,360 acres of the Tucson Mountain Park attached to Saguaro National Monument.

On December 31, 1975, forest service permits administered by the park service were no longer issued. Kenneth Kaecker, holder of the Tanque Verde permit, filed a civil suit on March 30, 1976, contending that he had perpetual grazing rights. The park service agreed to allow him to continue grazing until a court decision was reached. In 1979, Kaecker lost his suit, and grazing was ended on Saguaro National Monument. The monument became Saguaro National Park in 1994.

Saguaro National Park, which includes the Rincon Mountain and Tucson Mountain Districts, is home to the namesake giant saguaro cacti, barrel cacti, cholla cacti, and prickly pears, as well as quail, spotted owls, and javelinas. Each year, Saguaro National Park participates in conjunction with the National Geographic Society in a BioBlitz during an October weekend in celebration of biodiversity. Teams of scientists, schoolchildren, and volunteers stream across the park and attempt to identify as much of the flora and fauna as possible.

One

THE PARK AND POLITICS

For many years, the saguaro cactus stand east of Tucson attracted tourists and scientists, but until 1920, no effort was made to preserve these giant cacti. In 1928, University of Arizona president Homer Leroy Shantz commissioned John Harrison to purchase the rights on 480 acres of saguaro land for the university. Frank Hitchcock, publisher of the *Arizona Citizen*, approached Pres. Herbert Hoover with a view toward preserving the saguaro area as a national monument. Hoover agreed, and his executive proclamation made Saguaro a national monument on March 1, 1933. When Franklin D. Roosevelt became president, he transferred Saguaro National Monument to the National Park Service. National Park Service director Frank Pinkley wanted the mountain portion of Saguaro returned to the forest service. In 1945, the saguaros went through a bout of illness, and H.R. Tillotson, director of National Park Service Region 3, recommended abolishing the monument. Park service scientists ascribed the cactus disease to grazing and recommended that livestock be removed. Land settlements led to negotiations with the State of Arizona, Bureau of Land Management, and National Park Service in late 1948. There were 700 homestead applications to be examined. Assistant Secretary of the Interior Roger Ernst issued a public land order on August 25, 1959, by which 7,600 acres of the Tucson Mountain Park west of Tucson would be restored to mining. Secretary of the Interior Udall convinced Pres. John F. Kennedy to transfer part of the park to Saguaro by proclamation. On November 16, 1961, Kennedy issued a presidential proclamation enlarging Saguaro National Monument and creating the Tucson Mountain District. On October 14, 1994, Pres. William Clinton signed legislation that enlarged Saguaro's boundaries and made Saguaro National Park America's 52nd national park.

Dr. Homer Shantz is pictured in Saguaro National Park. The saguaro cactus (*Carnegiea gigantea*) defines the Sonoran Desert in southern Arizona and northern Mexico. These large, columnar cacti usually develop branches or arms as they age. They are covered with spines and have white flowers in the spring that bear red fruit in summer. Arizona has strict regulations regarding the harvesting, collection, or destruction of this species. Saguaros may live to be 150 to 200 years old, grow to be 40 to 60 feet tall, and weigh more than 3,000 pounds. (Courtesy University of Arizona Creative Center for Photography.)

On March 1, 1933, in the last days of his turbulent presidency and during the throes of the Great Depression, Pres. Herbert Hoover continued a tradition started by Teddy Roosevelt of designating public monuments. He signed a proclamation establishing Saguaro National Monument in the desert, east of Tucson, as a national public monument. It was a far-sighted accomplishment that would benefit future generations of Tucsonans and science. Saguaro became the first US national park or monument set aside to protect a plant species. (Courtesy Saguaro National Park.)

Born on January 30, 1882, in Hyde Park, New York, Franklin D. Roosevelt was stricken with polio in 1921. He became the 32nd president in 1933, and within a couple of weeks after taking office, he transferred several monuments, including Saguaro National Park, to the Department of the Interior. To guide the United States through the Great Depression, he established what came to be known as the alphabet agencies, such as the Civilian Conservation Corps (CCC), which carried out early construction work at Saguaro National Park. On June 10, 1933, President Roosevelt signed Executive Order No. 6166, which consolidated all national parks, national monuments (including Saguaro National Monument), national military parks, the 11 national cemeteries, national memorials, and the national capital parks into a single national park system. The National Park Service was directed to oversee all of these areas. This made the National Park Service the sole federal agency responsible for all federally owned public parks, monuments, and memorials. (Courtesy Roosevelt Library.)

In 1932, Harold L. Ickes supported Franklin D. Roosevelt for president. When he was appointed Secretary of Interior, Ickes stated, "The newspapers were taken by surprise and so was everyone else, myself included." Ickes took a special interest in the National Park Service and found himself in charge of the turbulent development of Saguaro National Monument. Ranchers were afraid of losing their grazing rights under the park service, but Ickes assured them that all valid rights would be respected. (Courtesy Roosevelt Library.)

The saguaro is covered with spines that protect the plant. When water is absorbed, the saguaro expands like an accordion, increasing the diameter of the stem and its weight. The saguaro may begin life in the shelter of a nurse tree or shrub, which provides a shaded, moist habitat. It grows slowly—as little as an inch a year—but to a height of 15 to 50 feet. (Courtesy University of Arizona Creative Center for Photography.)

Carl Trumbull Hayden served more than 40 years in Congress. During his long tenure, Hayden introduced several bills to establish the monument's boundaries. The *Los Angeles Times* wrote that Hayden had "assisted so many projects for so many senators that when old Carl wants something for his beloved Arizona, his fellow senators fall all over themselves giving him a hand. They'd probably vote landlocked Arizona a navy if he asked for it." (Courtesy Maricopa County Sheriff's Office.)

From left to right are Arizona's Sen. Henry Ashurst, Gov. John Phillips, and Rep. Carl Hayden. Carl Trumbull Hayden resigned as Maricopa County sheriff in 1912 to go to Washington, DC, as a representative from the newly established state of Arizona. He was elected to the senate in 1926, and a master plan for Saguaro National Monument was produced in 1947. A road was necessary, and Senator Hayden's assistance was enlisted to get an appropriation. The state had to relinquish control of its land as a prerequisite to construction of the road, and Hayden failed to gain the consent of the state land commissioner. (Courtesy Library of Congress.)

Isabella Greenway became Arizona's first congresswoman in 1933. Ten days after being elected, she met with Interior Secretary Harold L. Ickes. As she made her case for federal money for her state, Ickes said, "Mrs. Greenway, my time is very valuable. Can you compress all that Arizona wants onto one page?" She shot back, "Mr. Secretary, Arizona would never forgive me if I could get all it wanted onto one page." She grew up on a ranch and ran a ranch after her husband's death. She assured the Saguaro National Monument ranchers that they would retain their grazing rights under the park service. (Courtesy Arizona State Archives.)

Isabella Greenway entered politics as a delegate to the Democratic National Conventions in 1928 and 1932. A bridesmaid at Eleanor and Franklin D. Roosevelt's wedding, she seconded the nomination of Roosevelt to the presidency in 1932. Here, she poses with Eleanor and friends in front of the Arizona Inn in Tucson. (Courtesy Roosevelt Library.)

In a colorful career that included stints as an attorney, professional basketball player, and presidential candidate, Morris Udall made outstanding contributions to American conservation. Among his accomplishments as a representative from Arizona was securing passage of the Alaska Lands Act in 1980, which doubled the size of the national park system and tripled the amount of national wilderness. While in Congress, Udall ushered through landmark environmental laws, including the Strip Mining Reclamation Act, the Southern Arizona Water Rights Settlement Act, and the Tongass Timber Reform Act. His concern for the environment brought America a lasting gift of improved health for wild places and wild resources across the nation. (Courtesy Library of Congress.)

Pres. John Kennedy is announcing that Stewart Udall has been appointed Secretary of the Interior. The Udall brothers, Morris and Stewart, were both involved in getting the western stand of saguaros added to Saguaro National Park. In 1959, the Department of the Interior had issued an order that would have opened 7,600 acres to mining. The announcement met with loud protests. At public hearings, then-Arizona representative Stewart Udall said he would present legislation to make this part of the Saguaro National Monument. (Courtesy Library of Congress.)

A.E. Demaray entered government service in 1903 as a messenger in the Department of the Interior. Two years later, he was a draftsman in the Bureau of Reclamation. With the exception of an assignment as a civilian draftsman in the US Army of Pacification in Havana, Cuba, from March 1907 to December 1908, his entire career in the government had been in the Department of the Interior. He was determined that the park service should retain control of the Saguaro National Monument lands. (Courtesy Department of the Interior, National Park Service Historic Photograph Collection, Harper's Ferry Center.)

Arno Berthold Cammerer, the third director of the US National Park Service, was born in Nebraska in 1883. He went to Washington, DC, in 1904 to work as a bookkeeper and earned a law degree at Georgetown Law School. As director, he was determined that Saguaro National Monument would be managed by the park service. Cammerer felt development of Saguaro National Monument should be held to a minimum and that it should be used as a research reserve. (Courtesy Library of Congress.)

In September 1900, nineteen-year-old Frank Pinkley arrived in Phoenix. Pinkley had been sent to the Arizona Territory to recuperate from tuberculosis, but he would spend his lifetime with the National Park Service. Saguaro National Monument appeared for the first time in April 1934 in Pinkley's monthly report. Pinkley was told that a salary for a three-month temporary custodian would be provided starting July 1, 1934. (Courtesy Library of Congress.)

Fred Winn often found himself opposite those who wanted the Saguaro National Monument. Born in Madison, Wisconsin, he studied at Princeton and Rutgers. He became a rancher in Texas but returned to the east to study art. He moved to New Mexico, where he painted and illustrated western life. He joined the forest service in 1907 and served as ranger, assistant supervisor, and supervisor of the Apache, the Gila, and finally, the Coronado National Forest, where he was in charge from 1925 to 1942. To many people in southern Arizona, Fred Winn was the forest service. (Courtesy Shantz photographs, University of Arizona.)

Edgar Goyette provided leadership during the Great Depression. On January 16, 1941, Sen. Carl Hayden introduced a bill to revise the monument boundaries. Several Tucsonans, including University of Arizona president Alfred Atkinson, president of the Tucson Chamber of Commerce C. Edgar Goyette, forest supervisor Fred Winn, and James Converse, wrote to wish him a speedy passage. A calm, efficient man, Goyette had more friends and fewer critics than any other leader in Tucson's history. (Author's collection.)

Mayor Henry Jaastad wrote numerous letters on behalf of the Saguaro National Monument. Jaastad, an architect, served as Tucson mayor from 1933 to 1947. When the Tucson Garden Club completed its landscaping at the Padre Kino Park, Jaastad planted an ocotillo during a simple ceremony on March 15, 1939. Pictured are, from left to right, Jaastad with the ocotillo plant, Mrs. Alexander Murry, club president; Frank Lockwood, University of Arizona professor; Bishop Daniel Gercke, and Mrs. Fred Adams. (Author's collection.)

Joseph Frank Carithers was an accomplished horseman and member of the last of the horse cavalry units trained at Fort Riley, Kansas. His favorite walking stick was a piece of very prickly ocotillo. Carithers's articles were published in numerous magazines, and he revised the administrative standards handbooks for the National Park Service. Carithers believed in the conservation of America's resources and heritage for generations to come. His legacy includes the establishment of the western section of Saguaro National Park and serving as special assistant to Secretary of the Interior Stewart Udall during the Kennedy administration. (Courtesy Lynda Sánchez collection.)

Pictured here is Carithers and his wife, Hildegard, visiting with the widow of Pancho Villa, Luz Corral de Villa, at the museum in Chihuahua City while Carithers was superintendent at Big Bend. While serving as special assistant to Secretary of the Interior Udall, Carithers urged Udall to include the Tucson Mountain District in the Saguaro National Park because of the significance of the saguaro growth and the unusual petroglyphs. (Courtesy Lynda Sánchez collection.)

Pres. John F. Kennedy preserved an additional 15,000 acres, which included many magnificent petroglyphs in the Tucson Mountains, through presidential proclamation in 1961. Pres. Lyndon Johnson established the National Wilderness Preservation System by signing the Wilderness Act of 1964; Congress then legislatively mandated the preservation of wilderness values at Saguaro in 1976 by formally designating 71,400 acres as wilderness lands. (Courtesy Saguaro National Park.)

On October 14, 1994, Pres. William J. Clinton signed congressional legislation that enlarged the boundaries of Saguaro National Monument and made it America's 52nd national park. These presidential and congressional actions recognized that the significance of Saguaro National Park lies in the rich diversity of Sonoran Desert life found within a framework of historical and prehistoric human occupation. (Courtesy Clinton Library.)

Two

CRITTERS AND CACTUS VIEWS

Besides the magnificent saguaro, Saguaro National Park is home to many other desert plants and animals, including everything from the beautiful Gambel's quail to the Gila monster. The park hosted an event in 2011 known as the BioBlitz, which has been a great success. The 2011 National Park Service/National Geographic BioBlitz provided scientists, students, and citizens the opportunity to conduct a 24-hour inventory of the plants, insects, birds, and other living things that inhabit the desert park. Two days of round-the-clock exploration and documentation provided a snapshot of the many plants and animals in the 91,445-acre park. BioBlitz teams found at least 859 different species. These included more than 400 species, mostly invertebrate animals and nonvascular plants, previously unknown in the park, and at least one species of bryophyte, mosses, and liverworts believed to be new to science.

In the 1940s, conservation views were not as stringent, and the Tucson Sunshine Climate Club provided a series of photographic images of people dressed in cacti. Fortunately, places such as Saguaro National Park were established to protect cacti from this sort of action. Reginald "Reg" Manning's cartoons of cacti brought a smile to everyone's face. His book *What Kinda Cactus Izzat?* has gone through more than 40 printings.

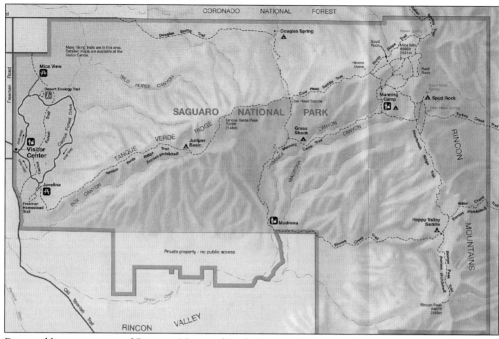

Pictured here are maps of Saguaro National Park Rincon Mountain District (above) and Saguaro National Park Tucson Mountain District (below). The park provides excellent maps designating the important sites, hiking and biking trails, and car-accessible roads. Saguaro National Park's two districts offer more than 165 miles (264 km) of hiking trails. A hike at Saguaro National Park can be a stroll on a short interpretive nature trail or a daylong wilderness trek. An overnight trip into Saguaro's wilderness can take one from an elevation of 3,000 feet to over 8,000 feet in about 15 miles. Hikes may began from any of five trailheads ranging from the easy-to-access Douglas Spring Trailhead at the east end of Speedway Boulevard to the more remote Italian Spring Trailhead, accessed through Reddington Pass in the adjacent Coronado National Forest. (Both, courtesy Saguaro National Park.)

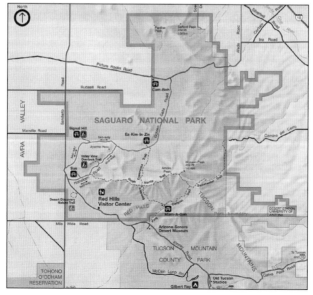

Rocky Mountain National Park assistant superintendent Ben Bobowski accepts the BioBlitz flag from Saguaro National Park superintendent Darla Sidles and John Francis from National Geographic. The festival offered an art program, which included pieces featuring local species created by local students, seniors, and artists. More than 100 poems and prose were written as part of a poetry inventory done with local scientists and writers. A poetry garden/walk displayed some of the submissions in their natural setting. (Courtesy Saguaro National Park.)

About 5,500 people, including more than 2,000 registered schoolchildren, participated in BioBlitz and the Biodiversity Festival. One of the great joys of the event was seeing children receive their degrees from Biodiversity University by participating in educational programs throughout the festival. (Courtesy National Geographic Society.)

Gambel's quails are common in southern Arizona and New Mexico, as well as in the Saguaro National Park. Look for these plump, volleyball-like birds running between cover on the open desert or posting a lookout on low shrubs. Like other quails, Gambel's quails have short necks, small bills, and square tails. Their wings are short and broad. Both sexes have a comma-shaped topknot of feathers on top of their small heads; it is fuller in the males than the females. (Courtesy WACC.)

Horned owls, with tufts of feathers that look like horns, love to nest in the saguaros and view the world from a lofty cacti platform. They vary in color from reddish brown to grey or black and white. Their underside is a light grey with dark bars, and a white band of feathers crosses their breast. Their large yellow eyes are usually rimmed by an orange facial disc. Their big feet are feathered to the ends of the toes, and the immature birds resemble the adults. (Courtesy US Fish and Wildlife Service.)

Mountain lions are solitary and shy animals seldom seen by humans. Mountain lions hunt primarily at night and rely on ambush to kill their prey. They prefer to stalk from above, using rock ledges and steep terrain. Males and females are territorial and often kill other lions found in their area. Uneaten portions of a kill are hidden or covered with leaves, dirt, or other debris. An entire deer can be consumed by an adult mountain lion in two nights. (Courtesy WACC.)

Javelinas, members of the peccary family, are hoofed mammals that originated in South America. The word *javelina* may have been derived from the Spanish word *javelin*, denoting their sharp tusks. They are common in central and southern Arizona. Their herds consist of two to 20 members, and they defend their territory, protect each other against predators, and interact socially. They are most active at night. Their coloration consists of speckled black, gray, and brown hair with a white collar around the shoulders. (Courtesy WACC.)

The Gila monster is a beautiful beaded lizard native to the Southwest, including Arizona and Sonora, Mexico. It is the only venomous lizard native to the United States and one of only two known species of venomous lizards in North America (the other being the Mexican beaded lizard). The Gila monster bite is venomous, but the lizard is very slow moving; nevertheless, it is best to stay out of the way of these lizards that make Saguaro National Park their home. It is protected by law in Arizona. (Courtesy WACC.)

Another critter that calls the park home is the skunk, legendary for its horrible-smelling spray. The spray is an oily liquid produced by glands under its large tail. Skunk spray causes no real damage to its victims, but it makes them uncomfortable. It lingers for several days and is very hard to remove. Predators typically give skunks a wide berth unless little other food is available. (Courtesy WACC.)

The white-winged dove has built her nest on the tip of a saguaro arm. Frequently, birds built their nests at the very top of a saguaro. It is fun to watch them knock the fruit to the ground and then start building their nests. (Courtesy WACC.)

From left to right are Hal Burns, a Tucson florist who made a replica of the *Spirit of St. Louis* when Charles Lindbergh visited Tucson on September 23, 1927; Sheriff James McDonald; Chief of Detectives Cliff Kronuer; attorney Kirke Moore; Charles Lindbergh; banker Harry H. Holbert; Undersheriff John Thomas; and Chief of Police Jack Dyer. Burns made the plane out of saguaro, ocotillo, and prickly pear and finished it off with a split barrel cactus for the nose. (Author's collection.)

Established in 1922, the Tucson Sunshine Climate Club was a welcome wagon and a promoter and fundraiser for all things Tucson. Tucson did not have much in the way of tourist accommodations, but it had plenty of saguaro cacti, so the idea was to produce ads showing Tucsonans innovatively wearing saguaro cactus. (Courtesy Saguaro National Park.)

This man in the image may have been thinking, "I hope my wife doesn't see this," while the woman seen here was probably wearing a skirt made of cactus ribs. Today, it is illegal to deface the saguaros, but at the time these photographs were taken, the Sunshine Climate Club did much good for Tucson by promoting its business potential and healthy climate. (Courtesy Saguaro National Park.)

Reg Manning's World War II and cactus cartoons earned him a Pulitzer Prize. He moved to Phoenix from Kansas and joined the *Arizona Republic* newspaper, which regularly carried his cartoons. His cactus cartoons included everything from the tiny pincushion cactus to the big-nosed saguaro. His advice was, "You'll enjoy the desert if you don't get stuck on it." (Courtesy Reganson Cartoon Books.)

Almost every large saguaro has holes in it. Reg Manning found a humorous way to teach folks about the saguaro apartments, which provide homes for a variety of birds. The woodpecker drills holes, and when it moves out, the wrens and a tiny elf owls takes over the second mortgage. (Courtesy Reganson Cartoon Books.)

Reg Manning's charming book *What Kinda Cactus Izzat?* has gone through at least 41 printings since 1941. With its many cactus characters, it is a who's who of the desert. The cactus belt of the United States is a place where almost every plant, including the lily, comes equipped with needles. (Courtesy Reganson Cartoon Books.)

It is hard to suppress a smile while looking at these dangerous desert desperados. While most desert plants are prickly, they bestow a lavish beauty—particularly the saguaro with its huge white waxy flower. The night blooming cereus shows off its white flower and delicious fragrance at night. The cereus flower, as big as a saucer when in full bloom, comes into flower once in the early morning hours and never blossoms again. Not only are many cactus fruits good to eat, the pads of the prickly pear sans stickers are canned and sold in grocery store as nopals. (Both, author's collection.)

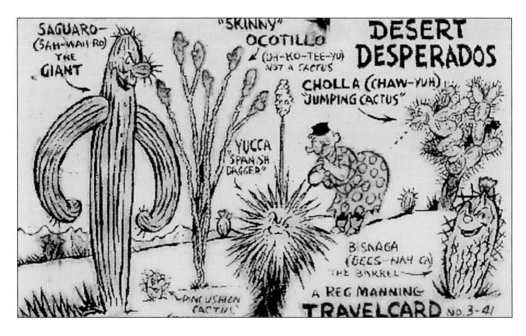

Arizona Wash and Dry

The friendly little saguaro is either greeting visitors or waving good-bye. The vegetation also introduces people to Arizona's mostly dry washes, except during the monsoons. (Author's collection.)

Three

THOSE WHO CAME BEFORE

Both Saguaro East and West are blessed with spectacular rock carvings, or petroglyphs. Rock paintings are called pictographs, while petroglyphs are made by incising directly on the rock surface using a stone chisel and a hammerstone. When the desert varnish on the surface of the rock was incised, the lighter rock underneath was exposed, creating the petroglyph. The Saguaro National Park petroglyphs may have been created by the Hohokam, ancestors of the present-day Tohono O'odham, probably from about 500 AD through the late 1680s. Petroglyphs may be religious symbols that reflect the cultures of the tribes and are central to the park's sacred landscape.

The Tohono O'odham traditionally harvest the saguaro fruit when it is ripe, usually in late June, for the *Nawait I'i* (Rain Ceremony) that occurs just before the monsoon season. The Tohono O'odham make candy, saguaro wine, jams, and jellies out of the fruit. Today, the Tohono O'odham purchase food by modern means, but historically, the saguaro provided a crucial source of nutritious food and drink when most other food sources were low because the desert was driest. Tribal members now teach workshops so that the saguaro harvest will not be forgotten

Tucson plumber and mayor George Julian and his young son explore picture rocks in 1914. This site near the Saguaro Park West contains hundreds of ancient rock symbols created mostly by the Hohokam, although some designs may date before 500 AD. The symbols include dancing human figures, animals, and abstract designs. Some appear to be markers for the equinoxes and the summer solstice. (Author's collection.)

Saguaro National Park's Signal Hill Petroglyphs may be the work of the ancient Hohokam, who may be the ancestors of the Tohono O'odham peoples in Southern Arizona. (Courtesy WACC.)

These American Indian symbols are thousands of years old and difficult to interpret. The specific meaning of the petroglyphs and why the ancient people created them is unknown. Art obviously played an important part in the religious lives of the Hohokam people. Possibly, for them, it captured things from a world beyond the rocks—the world inhabited by spirit creatures, in which dancers could travel in animal form, draw power, and bring it back for healing, rainmaking, and hunting game. Petroglyph maps may represent trails and symbols communicating time and distances traveled, as well as rivers, landforms and other geographic features. Realistic and abstract forms included stickmen, bighorn sheep, zigzags, spoked wheels, mazes, and the magnificent spiral at Signal Hill. The exact meanings of the rock art may never be known, so there will always be a mystery about places like Saguaro National Park. (Both, courtesy WACC.)

In 1942, Tohono O'Odham Joe Thomas and his wife and children bring the morning's harvest of saguaro fruit into their camp. Today, Stella Tucker is the last of the Tohono O'odham who conducts the sacred saguaro harvest on her family's ancestral camp. (Courtesy WACC.)

This Tohono O'odham woman is removing the Saguaro fruit by hooking it on a crossbar attached to a long saguaro pole. Today, the Tohono O'odham have cars and better roads, and they shop at the nearest grocery stores; however, once they and their ancestors, the Hohokam, were dependent the desert for their subsistence. (Courtesy WACC.)

This image of a Tohono O'odham woman was taken in 1907. The "puller" was constructed by tying two long saguaro ribs together with crosspieces attached at the top. Each of the saguaro crosspieces was tapered at each end to allow for insertion between the fruits. The Tohono O'odham would share the first fruits with the land by eating a portion and then placing a portion upon the earth. Only then would they harvest the fruit for themselves. (Courtesy Library of Congress, Edward S. Curtis.)

At the camp, the women clean the stones, sticks, and dirt from the fruit pulp, which is then dumped into a container of water and soaked for two or three hours. The mix is mashed by hand to blend the pulp with water. People drink the very sweet liquid from this mix after it has been boiled for one to two hours. (Courtesy WACC.)

Over the years, the method of harvesting the Saguaro fruit changed little from when this woman hooked the saguaro fruit in the 1930s. Burton Frasher created postcards and travelled the Southwest to find wonderful images such as this for his business. This particular saguaro is a readily recognizable icon of Saguaro National Park. (Courtesy Pomona Library, Burton Frasher Collection.)

The desert Indian tribes harvested not only the saguaro fruit but also other cacti, including the pads, or nopales, and as shown here, the fruit of the cholla cactus, which are also present in Saguaro National Park. The buds of the cholla, harvested in spring, are eaten as a vegetable and have a high calcium content. (Courtesy Library of Congress, Edwin S. Curtis.)

During the saguaro harvest moon, whole families of the Tohono O'odham used to camp out in Saguaro National Park, where the harvest of the saguaro fruit is still permitted. The bright red fruit is the size of a hen's egg and contains many tiny seeds to the delight of the desert birds. The Tohono O'odham would make candy, jelly, syrup, and wine from the fruit. (Courtesy Library of Congress, Edwin S. Curtis.)

In 1907, the Tohono O'odham women carried their *ollas*, or pots, on their heads and their other utensils in a woven burden basket. The basket, when placed on the ground, was supported by an easel constructed of saguaro ribs. (Courtesy Library of Congress, Edwin S. Curtis.)

In 1907, Edwin Curtis photographed these Qahatika women, who were once considered a subtribe of the Tohono O'odham, with their beautiful basketry. By harvesting the desert's plant and animal life, they lived a good life. When asked why they would not move to the fertile river valleys, they replied that their home was the best and that they did not have sickness like the river Indians. (Courtesy Library of Congress, Edwin S. Curtis.)

In this image, the Tohono O'odham women take a break. Note the burden basket propped up on a saguaro easel and the saguaro fruit puller propped against the saguaro. Metal bed frames and thin mattresses offer more comfortable sleeping arrangements than on the ground. Ramadas, covered in saguaro ribs, would provide shade over two tables, which doubled as eating and work areas. The photograph was taken in 1907. (Courtesy Library of Congress, Edwin S. Curtis.)

Two Tohono O'odham women cross the desert. One balances a basket of saguaro fruit on her head while the other carries the burden basket, known as a *kiho*, which contained the various tools needed for the saguaro harvest. (Courtesy Library of Congress, Edwin S. Curtis.)

The saguaro cactus provides its flowers, fruit, and seeds as an important food source for the desert fauna. It offers its sweet red fruit in June just before the desert rains, when the climate is at its driest and hottest. The birds pick the fruit off the saguaro top while animals on the ground scavenge for fallen fruits. (Courtesy University of Arizona Center for Creative Photography.)

The Tohono O'odham occupy numerous scattered villages. In 1907, their traditional houses were dome-shaped and thatched and featured flat roofs covered with earth. They were held together with saguaro ribs. Their basketry is among the finest. (Courtesy Library of Congress, Edwin S. Curtis.)

A Tohono O'odham woman fetches water from a community well. For many years, the tribe was referred to as the Papago, which means, "bean eaters," a demeaning term. Today, they are known by the name that they call themselves, Tohono O'odham, which means "desert people." (Courtesy Library of Congress.)

The photograph was probably taken in the late 1800s. Tohono O'odham women came into Tucson to sell their ollas, and buyers would fill the ollas with water and hang them in the breezeways to their homes. The wind blowing over the water was a primitive air-conditioning. Note the supports of the burden baskets, which are saguaro ribs. (Author's collection.)

A young Tohono O'odham woman takes pleasure in the Saguaro harvest. She would spend several days in the desert, harvesting saguaro fruit. During June and July, before the rains, the Tohono O'odham women rose early to collect the saguaro fruit and then spent the remaining daylight hours preparing, cleaning, and cooking it. (Courtesy Arizona State Museum, photographer Helga Teiwes.)

Juanita Ahil, above, had no electricity—just a wood-burning stove. Making cactus jam involves a series of steps of boiling the fruit and then straining the mixture and letting it dry. Historically, the mixture was used as a component of the rain ceremony, held in honor of the coming monsoon. Juanita Ahil died on January 23, 1994. Fortunately, her granddaughter, Stella Tucker, is keeping the tradition alive. (Courtesy Arizona State Museum, photographer Helga Teiwes.)

Four

RANCHERS AND MINERS

Before there was a monument or a park, there were ranchers. With the designation of a monument, ranchers who held land grazing permits from the forest service stood to lose their allotments and their homesteads. They had steadily increased the numbers of livestock until the region was overstocked with cattle that trampled the young saguaros. Most of the livestock were removed beginning in the late 1950s; however, by the mid-1970s, feral cattle began to appear on the monument. These animals caused vegetation damage, especially in the area around water holes. In 1976, Malcolm MacKenzie captured six bulls. A second attempt was made to remove these cattle in 1977. Two cattle were captured, and five died. Another effort was made in 1980, when 37 head were captured and one died. Finally, in 1984 and 1985, the remaining cows were shot, and all grazing on monument lands ceased. The Tanque Verde Ranch was not called by that name until it was acquired by James Converse in 1928. However, the Tanque Verde, or "Green Tank," name was known as early as 1860. A couple of large water holes covered with green algae are the source of the name.

Early mining is reflected in the limekiln ruins in both sections of the park. The two limekilns in the east unit are on the Arizona State Register of Historic Places. One kiln may have been built around 1880, and the second may have been constructed around 1910; both had ceased production by 1920. The Tucson Mountain District kilns were built in the mid-1890s. These crude kilns were built into an embankment so that the top was level with the embankment surface, which allowed the kilns to be easily charged with limestone and fuel from a wagon. The exposed area away from the embankment provided access for the lime removal. It took four days to make lime, during which time, wood would be added every two to three hours. Ten to fifteen cords of green palo verde or green mesquite would be burned within the span of those four days.

The Tucson Mountain District of Saguaro National Monument covers a portion of the Amole Mining District, which includes the Old Yuma Mine. It was sold to Epes Randolph in 1915. With expenses exceeding income, Randolph closed the mine in 1918. A group of New York financiers leased the Old Yuma Mine in 1920, and James Reilly, Harold K. Love, and T.P. Stines purchased the mine in 1923 and closed it in 1926. The Bureau of Land Management (BLM) Organic Act of October 22, 1979, required that all unpatented claims be refiled or they would be considered abandoned. Dick Jones refiled on the Old Yuma Mine, and in 1983, the Southwestern Mineral Associates purchased his claim and leased it to the Consolidated Mining and Milling Company. On May 3, 1983, the latter enterprise obtained permission from the BLM to operate a sodium cyanide leaching operation. The Tucson Mountain Association, out of concern over the potential effect of cyanide on the environment, worked successfully to prevent access to the mine. A portion of the Rincon Mining District covered the Rincon Mountain District of Saguaro National Monument. L. Martin Waer and partners filed mining claims, but in April 1901, they sold their claims to the Loma Verde Copper Company of Los Angeles, which closed the mine. Don Egermayer stated in his monthly report for March 1947 that he had caught two illegal prospectors on the monument.

Francisco Munguia located a claim on the parkland in 1875. He concentrated on irrigating his 30 acres and raising a few head of livestock. He relocated to Tucson and farmed along the Santa Cruz River. In 1885, Munguia lost his crops because Anglos had dammed the water upstream to furnish Silver Lake and the Chinese planted crops, which required a large amount of water. (Author's collection.)

Emilio Carrillo homesteaded a ranch on the parkland that came to be known as Las Cebadillas (Wild Barley). Today, this land outside the park boundary is the Agua Caliente Park. Carrillo had two hired men on the property to look after his 250 head of cattle. Several Tohono O'odham squatted on Carrillo's land and worked as day laborers. By 1900, Carrillo was a primary rancher with approximately 400 head of cattle. On May 7, 1904, bandits hanged Carrillo from the rafters in the museum room of the Tanque Verde Ranch. He told them that he had no money and somehow survived the torture, but he died four years later. His son and grandson would ranch in the park area. (Courtesy Arizona Historical Society.)

The Carrillos ranched on monument land for three generations. This picture shows, from left to right, Rafael, Emilio, Ysaura Leonor Carrillo and her baby, and Audelio Carrillo around 1910. Emilio Carrillo's permit had allowed him to graze 60 cattle on the forestland. His son, Rafael, was allowed the same number of cattle until the United States entered the First World War. In 1918, Rafael received an increased permit by which he could graze 265 animals. Rafael and Ysaura are buried in unmarked graves on the ranch cemetery. (Courtesy Arizona Historical Society.)

Cirilo León, shown here with his wife, Eloisa Ferrer, ranched in the Saguaro National Monument area. His land allotment is shown on an early map of the area. After the Gadsden Purchase in 1854, Tucson came under the jurisdiction of the United States. León's father, Francisco, was a lieutenant in the Mexican Army when the United States took possession of Tucson. León recalled that his father had built the walls of the Tucson presidio and had served in the Mexican military. (Author's collection.)

William Sanders Oury came to Tucson in 1856 after working the California gold fields. Oury served as Pima County sheriff from 1873 to 1877 and was the first president of the Arizona Historical Society. Around 1883, he moved to his Tanque Verde Allotment bordering the present Saguaro National Park, where he ran about 250 head of Kentucky-blooded cattle. He had grazing rights on what is now parkland. Most of the cattle were the product of crossbreeding either Hereford or Shorthorns with Mexican stock. These cattle could be fattened on the native gramma grass in an extremely short time. When asked why he didn't write history, Oury retorted, "I'm too damn busy making it." (Author's collection.)

Fall and Spring roundups were busy times at the Tanque Verde. The cowboys branded the livestock with a mark that identified the owner. The Emilio Carrillo brand was a stylized wine glass; Rafael Carrillo used "R/C," and the later Tanque Verde brand was "DW," which stood for "Desert Willow." The cowboy captured and secured an animal for branding by roping it, laying it over on the ground, tying its legs together, and applying a branding iron that had been heated in a fire. (Courtesy Tanque Verde Ranch.)

The cowboys who worked on the Las Cebadillas, seen in this c. 1920 photograph, did not let anything go to waste; they saved hair from the horses' manes and tails to make rope. Making rope involves a process similar to spinning yarn from wool. The mane hair makes a softer rope, while that of the tail is coarser. The strings are twisted in one direction, and the strands, consisting of four strings, are twisted together in the opposite direction. (Courtesy Arizona Historical Society.)

One of the approaches to Saguaro National Park is by Freeman Road, and there is a Freeman trail inside the park. The Homestead Act, signed by Pres. Abraham Lincoln on March 20, 1862, provided that the head of a family or anyone 21 years of age, whether a citizen or intended citizen, could take a quarter section of the public domain. If he lived upon and improved it for a period of five years, he could take title upon the payment of a fee. In 1929, Safford L. Freeman filed for a 640-acre homestead on land within the present-day park boundaries. He fulfilled the requirements of proving up by constructing a three-room adobe house, a "living corral" of ocotillos, and a well. (Courtesy Saguaro National Park.)

The members of the Safford Freeman family pictured here are, from left to right, Safford, Kirk, Ben, Mary, Tom, Shorty, Dorothy, Jean, and Bonnie. Ten individuals filed homestead patents between 1916 and 1930 within the area that would eventually become Saguaro National Park. One of these patents was filed by Safford and Viola Freeman, newlyweds from Georgia who had moved to Tucson in December 1913 and had been living on Sixth Street, which was rural and not much more than a cow trail at that time. However, Safford wanted to be even farther out. The Freeman claim for 640 acres was filed in the summer of 1929, and it was the next to last claim filed in Pima County. (Courtesy Saguaro National Park.)

In this c. 1944 image, Dorothy Freeman poses in front of a saguaro known as the "watermelon cactus" because of its many short, fat arms. This unusual saguaro cactus, which once stood at the park entrance, is no longer in existence. In 1951, the Freemans sold the property to the US government for $16,000, and it was integrated into the national monument. (Courtesy Saguaro National Park.)

Dorothy and Frank Freeman are photographed here. When the Freeman family moved in, there were no roads leading into the area. The Freemans and men from two other homesteads built a road that is now a large part of the Old Spanish Trail. The Freemans also improved their homestead by digging and dynamiting. They made their own adobe bricks to build their house, which measured 20 by 24 feet with a concrete floor. The dining room and kitchen were separate from the house, and there was a covered ramada between the two buildings. (Courtesy Saguaro National Park.)

The ranchers who had homesteaded on the parkland were very active in the racing circles. Here, Rukin Jelks poses with one of his winners at the Moltacqua Racetrack, located just a few miles from the parkland. It was the first quarter-horse racetrack in the United States. (Courtesy Department of Agriculture, University of Arizona.)

Visitors at the Moltacqua Racetrack in 1941 included, from left to right, Mrs. Rukin Jelks, rancher James Converse, Mrs. Converse, Mrs. Hubert Merryweather, Anson Lisk Jr., Hubert Merryweather, Mrs. Lisk, and Dennis Hunt. Hubert Merryweather was a tall, handsome man from Ohio who moved to Arizona in 1935. After attending the University of Arizona, he bought into Baca Float Ranch, Inc., serving as vice president before he enlisted in the Army and served for four years in the South Pacific during World War II. (Courtesy Department of Agriculture, University of Arizona.)

J. Rukin Jelks, shown here, is timing one of his racehorses. Jelks moved from Arkansas to the Tucson area in 1919 to attend the University of Arizona. He received both a bachelor's and a master's degree in animal husbandry and became a judge of champion cattle. He developed the quarter-horse racing industry on his X-9 Ranch, which covered several acres of the present-day Saguaro National Park near Tucson. (Courtesy Department of Agriculture, University of Arizona.)

James "Jim" Converse arrived at the Tanque Verde from Texas in 1928 when he purchased the Las Cebadillas Ranch from Rafael Carrillo and acquired the Tanque Verde Allotment. That same year, rancher Harry Wentworth died, and his wife sold the ranch and cattle to Converse. Converse was the first in the area to combine the idea of bringing paying guests to the ranch with raising cattle. He fought the premise of bringing land under the national park system because he was afraid he would lose the grazing rights for the 269 head of cattle he held under the forest service. By 1935, Converse was grazing 495 head of cattle. His first wife divorced him, and his second wife committed suicide. In 1945, during a drunken fight, Jim accidentally shot and killed ranch cowboy Francisco Romero. He was released from prison after a few years and died in 1969. He sold the Tanque Verde Ranch to Kenneth Kaecker. (Author's collection.)

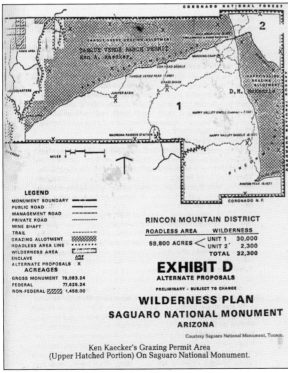

Ken Kaecker's Grazing Permit Area
(Upper Hatched Portion) On Saguaro National Monument.

Kenneth Kaecker was the last rancher to operate the Tanque Verde as a cattle ranch. He purchased the ranch from Jim Converse in 1956. Kaecker's grazing rights were diminished, and in 1973, he lost 40 calves to coyotes and mountain lions. Several of the area ranches exchanged ownership in the 1950s. Henry Jackson bought the X-9 in 1955. The ranch controlling the Pantano Allotment passed through several owners including Bill Veeck of baseball fame. In 1957, Brownie Cote, the father of the present owner, purchased part of the Tanque Verde land. Kaecker fought the grazing rule in the courts but eventually gave up. Kenneth Kaecker died in Tucson in 1997. (Author's collection.)

Nelson and Josephine Garwood purchased 480 acres of land within the present park boundaries in 1945. They built a house, a dam, and an airstrip. During World War II, Garwood worked on propellers at Davis Monthan Air Base and learned to fly. He earned a pilot's license and bought a plane. Garwood flew until he was 82 years old and gave up his license because of hearing loss. In 1955, the Garwoods sold their property, but the sales agreement stipulated that Nelson Garwood could use the airstrip for life. In the 1970s, the park service acquired the property through the right of eminent domain. The dam still stands, but today, only the foundations of the house and airstrip remain. The foundations are part of a park trail. (Courtesy Saguaro National Park.)

Some things never change, but the automobile was certainly an easier way of transporting hay for the horses at the Tanque Verde Ranch. In its most basic form, hay is dried grass and plants. (Courtesy Tanque Verde Ranch.)

Headin' Out 1950's

Here, a group of Tanque Verde guests ride out in the 1950s. James Converse started the idea of a dude ranch in the area to entice people to help him with ranch work. Today, guests at the ranch can learn how to ride. The ranch carries on with the spirit of the old west by providing guests with luxurious accommodations, fine dining, and an abundance of activities. Tanque Verde Ranch is nestled in the natural beauty of the Rincon Mountains, between Saguaro National Park and the Coronado National Forest. (Courtesy Tanque Verde Ranch.)

Sam Carr
Head Wrangler
1970-1981

Sam Carr served as the boss wrangler at the Tanque Verde for more than a decade. He achieved national recognition in the 1960s when his picture was chosen to represent the American cowboy in a leading Western magazine. Carr, born in Wyoming, spent most of his life catching wild horses, breaking them, and selling them to dude ranches and riding academies throughout the West. He once rode 70 miles just to take a lady to a dance. Carr said, "Horses are the way I make my living." (Courtesy Tanque Verde Ranch.)

Joe Valdéz not only served as a wrangler, he could also do almost any job that needed doing at the Tanque Verde. Wrangler is a term that describes someone who handles horses and cattle, but also pertains to those who handle guests at the ranch, some of whom ride and others who do not. Tanque Verde guest rides include trails into the Saguaro National Park. The wrangler takes guests on trails around Spud Rock, Mica Mountain, and a large bare outcropping known as Helen's Dome. For years, a German immigrant by the name of Bock raised potatoes in the area of Spud Rock. Helen's Dome was named for Helen Hackett, wife of a Captain Hackett who was stationed at Fort Bowie. Along with friends, she climbed the peak, and it was eventually named for her. (Courtesy Tanque Verde Ranch.)

Bob Cote, the current owner of the Tanque Verde Ranch, frequently leads guests on rides through Saguaro National Park. The ranch, which encompasses 60,000 acres, has changed hands only twice after Emilio Carrillo bought it in 1868. His family sold it to Jim Converse, who invited guests to participate in cattle roundups and ranch life. Brownie Cote from Minnesota purchased the ranch from Converse in 1957. He expanded the existing operation, which today is a world class resort managed by his son Bob Cote. (Courtesy Tanque Verde Ranch.)

BOB COTE
OWNER/MANAGER
1999

Early mining is reflected in the ruins of the limekilns within the park. The two limekilns in the Rincon Mountain District have been placed on the Arizona State Register of Historic Places. Lime produced in Saguaro National Park may have been used in the wall on the Park Avenue side of the University of Arizona. The Tucson Mountain District kilns were built in the mid-1890s, and by 1910, the kilns no longer functioned. In mid-1896, the *Tucson Citizen* reported that Juan Romero had died while working at his kiln, situated about three miles from Tucson. As for the west section kilns, a 1920 publication stated that limestone on the west side of that range had been used for many years to manufacture lime, but none had been burned for some time. (Courtesy Saguaro National Park.)

James Lee developed the Nequilla Mine, the first mine to be patented in the Amole District. The Nequilla was discovered on December 11, 1865. Jesus and Ramon Bustamente and Domingo Gallego recorded their claim on February 17, 1866. Two partners sold their interest to James Lee and William Scott in 1867. When Lee and Scott patented their claim on September 28, 1872, it was the first mining claim to be patented in Arizona Territory. Apache raids in 1867 resulted in the death of a cowboy and the loss of livestock. In the 1870s, miners extracted silver ore, which they shipped to a San Francisco smelter via Guaymas, Mexico. Lee and Scott operated their mine until the depression forced them to close in the early 1880s. At that time, they had reportedly produced $70,000 in silver. (Author's collection.)

Pictured here from left to right are Mrs. Breathert, Tucson librarian; A.J. Temple, railroad man; Mrs. Epes Randolph; and Epes Randolph. Epes Randolph invested in many Tucson businesses, including ranching and mining, in the Amole Mine area of Saguaro National Park. Randolph came to Tucson in 1856 seeking relief from tuberculosis. He was a railroad executive and civil engineer. He became chancellor of the University of Arizona and vice president of the Consolidated Bank of Tucson. The Old Yuma Mine was purchased in November 1914 for $50,000 by W.J. Laffey. He intended to mine molybdenum but evidently changed his mind and sold the property to Epes Randolph in 1915. Randolph constructed a mill that could handle 100 tons of ore a day. Some molybdenum was obtained from the mine, but not enough to draw attention. With expenses exceeding income, Randolph closed the mine in 1918. (Courtesy Arizona Historical Society.)

Frederick "Fritz" Contzen was born in Germany in 1831. His father was the chief forester on an estate belonging to the Prince of Waldeck. Contzen came to the United States at the age of 14 with his older brother Julius. In Galveston, Texas, they joined the Texas rangers. Fritz's ranch, located near San Xavier Mission, was known as Punta de Agua. He arrived in Arizona in 1854 as a member of the boundary commission. Contzen Pass, where Picture Rocks Road crosses the Tucson Mountains, was named for him. He became good friends with Emilio Carrillo, and they each married a Ferrer sister. (Author's collection.)

Marguerita Ferrer Contzen, wife of Fritz, wears the Star of Waldeck, which was presented to her by Prince Georg of Waldeck. When Fritz and Marguerita visited Germany, her father-in-law presented her to the court of Wilhelm I, King of Prussia. (Author's collection.)

Philip Contzen, the son of Fritz and Marguerita Contzen, served for many years as a Tucson surveyor and drafter. In this picture, he is shown as a member of Company D of the Arizona National Guard. In September 1897, Philip Contzen found an old limekiln while surveying subdivision lines in township no. 14, range no. 16. He found the limekiln at the site of the remnants of the two kilns in the Rincon Mountain District of Saguaro National Park. It was not in operation at the time. He did not provide a construction date. (Author's collection.)

Charles Shibell was part owner in the Cymbeline Mine in the Amole District of Saguaro National Park. He tried his hand at ranching and mining and became Pima County sheriff from 1877 to 1881. In 1881, Shibell became proprietor of Tucson's Palace Hotel, and he served many years as Pima County recorder. He died in 1908. (Author's collection.)

Pictured are William Zeckendorf with his wife, Julia, and children. William Zeckendorf, a Tucson Jewish pioneer and merchant, bought the Cymbeline Mine from Charles Shibell. Zeckendorf also served as a member of the Eighth Legislature of Arizona. In 1893, Zeckendorf showed off Arizona products at the Chicago World's Fair. The products included ribs of saguaro and cholla cacti. (Author's collection.)

A group of New York financiers purchased the Old Yuma Mine in 1923. The investors included Harold K. Love, pictured here with the famous Buntline special. Love is best known for his support of Tombstone, Arizona. Love, James Reilly, and T.P. Stines formed the Arizona Concentrating Minerals Recovery Company and announced their intent to install machinery that would permit them to further develop the property. Love and Stines lost interest and left the company, so Reilly reorganized the business as the International Ore Separation Company. He shipped one railroad car of ore by June 1924 and had another ready for transport. (Author's collection.)

The pioneer Van Alstine family is buried in the Tanque Verde Cemetery, located on the Las Cebadillas Ranch. By 1880, the Campos, Van Alstine, Oury, and Carrillo families ran more than 1,200 head of cattle on public rangelands that would become Saguaro National Park. William Van Alstine (1818–1898) squatted on land on which he had 40 acres under cultivation, and he owned 350 head of cattle, most of which he pastured in the San Pedro Valley during the winter and spring. Some of his cows formed a small dairy herd. In 1887, Van Alstine, along with several other pioneers, served as pallbearers at William Oury's funeral. (Both, author's collection.)

Five

STEWARDS OF THE PARK

It is one thing to designate a monument or park, but it is quite another to set in motion its care for eternity. Saguaro National Park benefited greatly from the Civilian Conservation Corps (CCC), which, during the Great Depression of the 1930s, constructed many of the structures standing today. The CCC was a public work relief program that operated from 1933 to 1942 in the United States for unemployed, 18- to 25-year-old unmarried men from relief families. The CCC provided unskilled manual-labor jobs related to the conservation and development of natural resources in lands owned by federal, state, and local governments. The CCC was designed to provide employment for young men who had difficulty finding jobs during the Great Depression while also implementing a general natural resource conservation program in every state and territory.

There are many National Park Service employees, as well as invaluable volunteers, who take care of America's natural resources. Though it is impossible to recognize everyone involved with Saguaro National Park, this chapter presents the high-caliber people involved in the park. The following people once served as custodian or superintendent of Saguaro National Park (from 1948 on, the term *custodian* was changed to *superintendent*): Charles Powell, 1934–1935; Don W. Egermayer, 1939–1942 and 1946–1948; Ira John Peavy, 1942–1944; Paul L. Beaubien, 1944–1946; Samuel A. King, 1948–1953; John G. Lewis, 1953–1956; J. Barton Herschler, 1956–1958; John O. Cook, 1959–1962; Monte E. Fitch, 1962; Paul A. Judge, 1962–1965; Robert L. Giles, 1966–1968; Harold R. Jones, 1968–1972; Quincy B. Evison, 1972–1973; Richard H. Boyer, 1973–1975; William M. Lukens, 1975–1980; Ross R. Hopkins, 1980–1982; Robert L. Arnberger, 1983–1987; William Paleck, 1987–1992; Doug Morris, 1993–1998; Frank Walker, 1999–2008; Sarah Craighead, 2009–2010; and Darla Sidles, 2011–present.

Because of Shantz's efforts, the Tanque Verde Camp was established in July 1935. Camps were constructed by local men chosen by the Pima County Reemployment Committee. Buildings included four barracks, a mess hall, a kitchen, a recreation hall, officers' quarters, a hospital, a latrine, and shower rooms. The operation was overseen by the Army, which provided the commanding officer, physician, and educational adviser. The park service approved and supervised the work projects. The desk pictured was used by the commanding officer. (Courtesy Colossal Cave.)

Funds were provided by the park service for the establishment of CCC camps in and near what later became both units of Saguaro National Monument. Pima County, which operated the Tucson Mountain Park, applied for two camps in August 1933. In 1935, University of Arizona president Homer L. Shantz requested a camp to be established on the university-controlled land within the monument. Pictured is the mimeograph machine that workers from the camp printed their newsletter on. (Courtesy Colossal Cave.)

During the summer, CCC workers were usually transferred to more northerly destinations, such as the Grand Canyon. One exception was made during the 1934–1935 drought period, when extra funds were allotted to hire more young men in the CCC drought camps, like those at Saguaro National Park. (Courtesy Arizona Historical Society.)

CCC workers such as G. Johnson (left) and Jimmy Banks built roads, trails, and picnic areas with ramadas, fire pits, tables, and restrooms at the park. They also constructed check dams, four windmills, and water catchments for wildlife. Enrollment usually ranged from 150 to 200, but the camp was not occupied on a year-round basis. (Courtesy Arizona Historical Society.)

Don Egermayer and his wife, Ruth, arrived at Saguaro National Park in the fall of 1939 while driving a 1933 Chevrolet with 133,000 miles on it. Egermayer's budget to run the park until the following July was $60. His duties included keeping the loop road graded, so he constructed a drag with two railroad ties, 12 feet long, pulled by his pickup. One of Egermayer's special memories was a visit by John D. Rockefeller. Egermayer and his wife were cremated, and their ashes were brought to Saguaro National Park. (Courtesy WACC.)

Ruth Egermayer, pictured here, did just about everything at the park. Ruth and Don's first home was an abandoned former CCC tool shed. Its roof leaked so badly that birds could fly in and out. Don brought in water from Tucson's Randolph Park in two 10-gallon cans. Coleman lanterns provided the lighting, and communication was by shortwave radio. There was no indoor plumbing. (Courtesy WACC.)

Ruth handled everything from rounding up firefighting crews to banding birds, as she is seen doing here. She was also a crack marksman with small-bore guns. Once, when Ruth pointed out signs saying "Private" and "No ranger on duty" to a female visitor, she responded, "But I am from New York. I don't read signs." In 1940, the CCC built a three-room combination visitor center/custodian house at the monument. It had a living room, kitchen, and office but no electricity or plumbing—that came after World War II. (Courtesy WACC.)

Ira John Peavey served as custodian of Saguaro National Park from 1942 to 1944. He is holding a young javelina. There is little doubt that he was fond of the park's wildlife. This was a time when the custodian was expected to be available at all times to escort and educate visitors. (Courtesy WACC.)

This is a farewell party for John G. Lewis in 1956. During Lewis's tenure, the visitor list reached 40,000 per year, and the park became known as the Valley of the Marching Giants. Also during this time, a new $23,500 administration building was dedicated. The staff included Supt. John G. Lewis, ranger Benjamin Zerbey, foreman-packer Frank Stansberry, and maintenance man Donovan Lathrop. (Courtesy WACC.)

Supt. J. Barton Herschler saw Saguaro National Monument celebrate its 25th anniversary in 1957, a year that saw 133,625 visitors. Herschler was born on March 21, 1897, in Ashland, Ohio. In 1929, he became a park ranger at Yosemite, and in 1938, he transferred to Rocky Mountain National Park as chief ranger. In 1955, Herschler transferred to Millerton Lake Recreation Area, and in 1957, he went to Saguaro National Monument in Arizona as superintendent. In 1958, he retired. Here, Herschler presents an award to Frank Stansberry. The cart in the foreground was used for stringing barbed wire fence. (Courtesy WACC.)

Supt. John O. Cook had much to smile about in his new air-conditioned office. With the celebration of the 25th anniversary, a cactus forest fete was scheduled. There were special auto caravan tours with stops at special habitats, along with colorized motion pictures showing the area's wildlife. Park rangers talked about the saguaros and other plants during the caravan's stops. (Courtesy WACC.)

Supt. John O. Cook is pictured here in the formal uniform of the Saguaro National Monument. By the 1950s, the monument was requesting that all cars stop by the new administration building and sign in so that it could get an accurate count of the visitors. (Courtesy WACC.)

The park's firefighting crew is seen here in 1958. Pictured from left to right are Don Marley, an engineer from the National Park Service's World Office of Design and Construction (WODC); Andy Kemmerer, head fire control; Mike Escalante, laborer; Bill Wilder, fire control aid; Ray Foust, fire control aid; Dan Griffith, crew boss; Jim Carroll, laborer; and two unidentified. Kemmerer went on to become director of the National Marine Fisheries Service. Ray Foust started his long career with the National Park Service as a seasonal firefighter at Saguaro National Park in 1958. In his 36 years with the agency, he went on to work at remote and urban parks from a Montana lake to the Statue of Liberty. (Courtesy WACC.)

Supt. John Cook witnessed growth and change at Saguaro National Park, but he always considered his interaction with visitors, explaining the park's unique plant life, one of his most important duties. (Courtesy WACC.)

This picture of the Saguaro National Monument staff was taken on March 1, 1959, the monument's Establishment Day. Pictured from left to right are Supt. John Cook, George Olin, Frank Stansberry, Barbara Chisay, Donovan Lathrop, Earl Fanner, William T. Krueger, and W. Lowell White. White went to become the superintendent of North National Cascades Park in Washington. (Courtesy WACC.)

Superintendent Cook gives an award to Donovan Lathrop as chief ranger Bob Morey holds the "Men Working" sign. Lathrop was a longtime, hardworking fixture at the monument. (Courtesy WACC.)

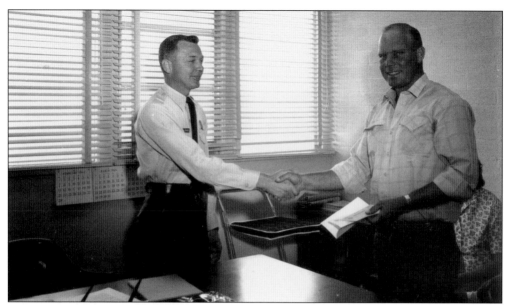

Chief ranger Bill Dyer presents foreman George Hanley with a performance award. (Courtesy WACC.)

In this image, chief ranger Bill Krueger awards Frank Stansberry a $150 check for his "sustained, superior performance." From 1947 to 1959, Stansberry and his animals made a total of 95,000 miles without loss of property or injury to the animals. Stansberry's horse Blaze supervises the ceremony. (Courtesy WACC.)

Bob Morey began working in Yellowstone as a "smoke chaser" in 1943 and stayed through 1952, when he took a job as ranger with Saguaro National Monument. In 1963, Morey went on to work at Badlands National Park, finishing his career at Yellowstone National Park. (Courtesy WACC.)

Supt. Barton Herschler (left) presents an award to Donovan Lathrop. In the background are, from left to right, engineer Don Marley from WODC, chief ranger Ben Zerbey, and head of maintenance Frank Stansberry. (Courtesy WACC.)

Regional director H.R. Tillotson stands at the far right while Saguaro National Monument superintendent Lewis talks about saguaro cactus with Hugo Miller (left) and regional park service director Tim Allen (second from left). With the constant fights over grazing rights and homesteads, the park service was ready to abandon the monument in 1949. Fortunately, the City of Tucson helped stave off this action. At one point, Tillotson recommended abolishing the monument, but Arno Demaray responded that Tillotson should not give up. Tillotson had a long career in the park service, and this may be the last photograph of him. (Courtesy WACC.)

During the early 1930s, National Park Service director Horace Albright concentrated his efforts on expanding and rounding out the National Park System. Even as early as 1932, a need was seen to have park service buildings that blended with the environment. This building is very utilitarian, but it does have a window cooler, a real luxury in southern Arizona's hot summers. (Courtesy WACC.)

This building, probably constructed by the CCC, stood at the north boundary of the park in 1949. However, with a water tank and windmill, it probably served as the park headquarters at one time. (Courtesy WACC.)

Unfortunately, vandalism has always been a problem in national parks. In this photograph, a ranger poses with a hauler's truck full of wood. Due to the theft of this wood, a considerable amount of living plants, situated in one of the best sections of the park, were trampled and smashed. In the 1800s, Emilio Carrillo was caught chopping wood in the park area. When the CCC arrived in the 1930s, it often used confiscated wood in its construction projects. (Courtesy WACC.)

According to environmentalists, the unnatural footprint left by Saguaro National Park's visitors is growing, as is the case with all national parks. Hikers wander off marked trails and trample vegetation. From its inception as a park, Saguaro employees have had to deal with car problems and other unintentional issues. Vehicles clog park roads and contaminate the air with tailpipe emissions. Bicycle accidents are also on the rise. Tourists leave behind water bottles and other litter. The more egregious problem is those vandals who deliberately destroy the saguaro and other plants. (Courtesy WACC.)

Fire in the park is always of concern. In 1933, the Manning Camp area was established as part of Saguaro National Park and began its usage as a base of operations for the firefighters. The park service uses the cabin for fire and trail crews. Around 1958, supplies were brought into the camp by simply pushing them out the door of the plane toward a target area. Today, the cabin provides an important base for prescribed burn operations. (Courtesy WACC.)

In 1955, park firefighters enjoy a break and meal around a campfire. They are, from left to right, Bob Zerbey, Frank Stansberry, packer; Donovan Lathrop, laborer; and unidentified. Today, controlled burning is recognized as a necessary part of nature to allow the plants to achieve their maximum potential. Nature is nurtured by fire, which clears away clogged vegetation and stimulates new growth. (Courtesy WACC.)

The packer in the foreground is Mike Escalante, and the one toward the rear is Jim Johnson. The two water tanks at the Manning Camp were filled by packing and hauling over a go-devil, a rough one-mile stretch of trail from the meadow to the Manning Camp. In 1958, this was considered a primitive method, but it was still utilized during that time. (Courtesy WACC.)

Maintenance chief Frank Stansberry (left) and Neil Bunsly were especially adept at using horses and mules to accomplish their work. (Courtesy WACC.)

Saguaro National Park museum aide Dee Dodge teaches Tucson Girl Scouts about desert life. It is obviously windy, but the girls seem focused on learning about cacti. Early park service women's uniforms were controversial; some didn't like the men's style shirt and thought that a sports blouse should be substituted instead, while others believed that one of the hats made them look like stewardesses. (Courtesy WACC.)

Marjorie Cunningham started her park service career by selling tickets at the Grand Canyon. It was thought to be too demeaning for men to perform this task. She later went to work at Saguaro National Park West, where she maintained a scrapbook of newspaper articles about the park's activities. Today, Cunningham has her own law firm in Tucson. (Courtesy Marjorie Cunningham.)

Barbara Lund, a Saguaro Park naturalist, inspects the saguaro exhibit commemorating the 50th anniversary of the establishment of the National Park Service. Lund wrote several natural history articles on the park's plant life. (Courtesy WACC.)

On September 12, 1965, Saguaro National Park held a retirement party for Supt. Paul Judge at the Casa Molina Restaurant in Tucson. His wife, Frances, opens their gift of an electric blanket. (Courtesy Saguaro National Park.)

In this August 25, 1966, image, Robert L. Giles celebrates the 25th anniversary of the establishment of Saguaro National Monument. Pictured from left to right are chief ranger Gunzel, chief naturalist Warren Steenburgh, Mrs. Giles, Maureen Giles, Supt. Robert Giles, naturalist Strandburgh, secretary Gonzaliez, and assistant May. Robert Giles served as superintendent of Saguaro National Park from 1966 to 1968. He was the recipient of the Distinguished Flying Cross for extraordinary heroism during a bombing flight over Germany on April 18, 1944. During World War II, Giles was wounded when his plane was shot down, and he spent a year in a German prisoner of war camp. (Courtesy WACC.)

In 1948, Giles began his career with the National Park Service with an assignment to Zion National Park. His next assignments included Mesa Verde National Park and Rocky Mountain National Park in Colorado, Big Bend National Park in Texas, and the regional office in Santa Fe, New Mexico, where he reached the rank of chief of budget and finance. (Courtesy Kirtland Air Force.)

Saguaro National Park superintendent Harold Jones hosted a visit by several park officials on September 12, 1968. From left to right, they are Western regional director John Rutter, Southwest regional director Frank Kowski, Midwest regional director Fred Fagergren, National Park Service director George Hartzog, and Superintendent Jones. Hartzog, the seventh National Park Service director, held that position from January 1964 until December 1972. Jones would go on to work at the Agate Fossil Beds in Nebraska. (Courtesy WACC.)

Robert Arnberger is a second-generation park service employee who followed his father in a proud career. Now, his son works at Saguaro National Park. Robert was born at Grand Canyon, on the south rim, in a two-room clinic while his father was called away to fight a small forest fire. He worked at the Grand Canyon as superintendent as well as at Saguaro National Park. Arnberger completed his career as regional director of Alaska, which covered more than 54 million acres of the nation's wildest land. (Courtesy Robert Arnberger.)

In 1984, Rob Arnberger and Saguaro National Park, along with the Tucson Mountain Association, the Sierra Club, and the Tucson Mountain Park, worked successfully to stop Consolidated Mining Company from operating a cyanide leech process to extract gold from a mine on the border of Saguaro National Park Tucson Mountain District. This land was part of the historical Amole Mining District. The few cattle left on the Saguaro National Park Rincon Mountain District had gone feral and presented a danger to visitors. Arnberger killed the last of the old cows. So, after more than 100 years, two of Saguaro National Park's concerns—cattle grazing and mining—were effectively solved. (Courtesy Robert Arnberger.)

Doug Morris served as a park superintendent for 13 years, first at Saguaro National Park in Tucson, Arizona, and then at Shenandoah National Park. For the last three years of his assignment at Saguaro National Park, Morris served concurrently as the acting chief of the WACC. Morris was often assigned to develop new NPS policies. In 1999, he spent three weeks meeting with government officials and park staff/community leaders in Kenya and Tanzania. For four years, he served as a key NPS representative advancing implementation of a partnership between the US National Park Service and the EUROPARC Federation, an organization that includes managers of parks from throughout Europe. Since retirement, Morris continues to work in the international arena. He twice visited China on behalf of the Global Heritage Fund to advise the development of quality visitor experiences in the ancient city of PingYao in Shanxi Province. (Courtesy Shenandoah National Park.)

During the summers of 1967 and 1968, while working out of Manning Camp near the top of the Rincon Mountains, William Paleck learned many of the skills that formed his foundation as a park ranger. Through experience, he learned how to pack a mule, fall a tree, put out a fire, get along with seven other guys in tight quarters, cook their meals for a week without making anyone sick, rescue injured Boy Scouts, and rebuild a Briggs & Stratton engine. During his tenure as superintendent at Saguaro, Paleck learned how to deal with news media, delegate responsibility to those who could handle it, and value the fact that while his job was important, he was not. He said, "I don't think I could have contributed what I did as a manager in the National Park Service during the subsequent fifteen years without that foundation." (Courtesy William Paleck.)

In this photograph, Bill Paleck studies a model of the new building at Saguaro National Park Tucson Mountain District. Paleck grew up in Tucson, Arizona, where he graduated from the University of Arizona. He began working for the National Park Service in 1967 as a seasonal trail laborer at Saguaro. Paleck was a park ranger at the Home of Franklin D. Roosevelt and Vanderbilt Mansion National Historic Sites in Hyde Park, New York, and served as chief of interpretation and resources management at Wupatki and Sunset Crater National Historic Sites in Arizona. He also served as park ranger in the Alaska Regional Office. In 1987, he was selected as superintendent of Saguaro National Monument. During his tenure, Paleck forged constructive relationships with county and municipal governments and the development industry during a period of explosive population growth in southern Arizona. He went on to become superintendent of the North Cascades NPS Complex. Recent honors include awards from the Pima County Planning and Zoning Commission, Mayor of Tucson, Arizona, and the Pacific West Region. Since retirement, Paleck has become a Washington State and Superior Court–certified mediator. Today, he practices facilitative, interest-based mediations in divorce, parent/teen, workplace, contract, and foreclosure cases. (Courtesy Saguaro National Park.)

During Franklin Walker's tenure as superintendent, Saguaro National Park developed an agreement with the Tucson BLM Field Office to share facilities and opportunities. This resulted in the construction of the Broadway Trailhead. The Friends of Saguaro acquired a ceramic tile wall that depicted a slice of the Sonoran Desert at the Red Hills Visitor Center. The park participated in the largest multispecies habitat conservation plan in the United States. During Walker's tenure, Saguaro National Park fire facilities were designed to improve safety for the helibase operation and provide critical space for the fire management team. The Arizona Site Stewards program helped monitor the 350 archeological sites in the park. Throughout his career, Walker has served on many prestigious committees, including: National Park Service representative on the Pima County Sonoran Desert Conservation Plan; member of the University of Arizona School of Renewable Natural Resources Advisory Council; and member of the 1999 Congressional Bridge Team to orient new members of Congress to the National Park Service. He has also presented talks about the park for the Aldo Leopold Conference in Madison, Wisconsin. (Courtesy Franklin Walker.)

Sarah Craighead went on to become the superintendent of Death Valley National Park in 2009 after leaving Saguaro National Park. She worked as a park ranger at Washita Battlefield National Historic Site, Acadia, Carlsbad Caverns, and the Grand Canyon, as well as Mesa Verde National Park, Manassas National Battlefield Park, and Independence National Historical Park. A graduate of Transylvania University, Craighead recalled, "Of all of the things that the Saguaro National Park staff worked on while I was Superintendent there, I am most proud of our efforts to protect Wilderness and Wilderness values. As a park largely composed of Wilderness lands surrounded by an urban landscape it was often difficult to keep the solitude and natural quality of Wilderness lands intact, especially those on the fringes of the park where development bumped into the boundaries. The staff worked tirelessly to insure that we did everything possible so that generations of Americans decades from now will have the opportunity to find a place of renewal and natural beauty." (Courtesy Sarah Craighead.)

Darla Sidles became superintendent of Saguaro National Park in 2011. Sidles worked closely with park staff and partners on issues such as planning for the President's House, the completion of the Independence Mall redevelopment plan, and updating security procedures at Independence National Park in Philadelphia. Sidles also served at Grand Canyon Parashant National Monument in Arizona. Sidles began her career as a student conservation association volunteer in 1986 with the US Forest Service in the North Cascades. In 1992, Sidles became a seasonal biological technician at Zion National Park. During her Zion years, Sidles also worked as a legislative fellow to Sen. Daniel Akaka (HI) in Washington, DC. (Courtesy Darla Sidles.)

Six

THE PEOPLE AND THE PARK

Long before there was a park, the people came to walk, ride, and drive through the forest of the giants. They were hikers, photographers, scientists, and the curious who asked nothing more than to enjoy the desert's special beauty. In 1934, there were 2,500 visitors, but now, more than 700,000 tourists visit Saguaro National Park annually. The park is composed of the Rincon Mountain District and the Tucson Mountain District. Park facilities include 150 miles of hiking trails and shorter walking trails with interpretative information available. Tucson Mountain District is west of Tucson, Arizona, while the Rincon Mountain District is east of the city. Both districts were formed to protect and exhibit forests of the saguaro cactus. The Tucson Mountain District of Saguaro National Park ranges from an elevation of 2,180 feet to 4,687 feet and contains desert scrub and desert grassland. The district's average annual precipitation is approximately 10.27 inches. The Rincon Mountain District of Saguaro National Park ranges from an elevation of 2,670 feet to 8,666 feet and contains desert grassland, oak woodland, pine-oak woodland, pine forest, and mixed conifer and has an average annual precipitation of approximately 12.30 inches. As guardian of the signature plant, the park conducts saguaro censuses, and in 2010, it counted more than 17,000 saguaros. In some areas, the number of saguaros has more than doubled since 1990. Increased usage of the park means increased unnatural footprints in the area. Time in Saguaro National Park is time spent in a special place. As Homer Shantz said, "The full richness of the experience is so profoundly enhanced by that sense."

These two women enjoy a Sunday carriage ride through the park in the late 1800s. There is little doubt that many a carriage wheel was broken on the rough terrain. (Courtesy Saguaro National Park.)

In this 1877 image, a woman in a handsome riding outfit sits sidesaddle and smiles for George Rothrock's camera. Rothrock was born on March 31, 1843, in Jefferson City, Missouri, the eldest son of German emigrants. In May 1877, he set out on a photographic odyssey that took him from Phoenix through the Pima Reservation to Sacaton, on to Florence, and then Camp Lowell outside Tucson in August 1877. He became well known for his stereopticon images. (Courtesy Saguaro National Park.)

G. H. ROTHROCK.   PHOENIX, ARIZONA.

Old automobiles plowed through the desert with little concern that they were sure to have a tire puncture before they reached their destination; nor could the passengers have been too comfortable in the broiling sun with the car's top down. Today, with the park so close to the city, automobile emissions have a definite negative impact on Saguaros. (Courtesy Arizona Historical Society.)

91

This unnamed, well-dressed gentleman is wearing a long-sleeved white shirt, tie, jodhpurs and sturdy hiking boots. The picture provides a good indication of the size of the saguaros in relation to the man. (Courtesy WACC.)

Homer Shantz loved all things plants. Dr. Shantz, born in Michigan in 1876, was educated at Colorado College and received his PhD from the University of Nebraska in 1905. He held many important positions during his lifetime, including as a researcher with the Department of Agriculture, head of the botany department of the University of Illinois, president of the University of Arizona from 1928 to 1936, botanist in the division of wildlife management for the US Forest Service, and the guiding light in the establishment of the Saguaro National Monument, which later became Saguaro National Park. (Courtesy University of Arizona Creative Center for Photography.)

Homer Shantz, the 10th president of the University of Arizona, spent nearly six decades traveling the world and taking thousands of photographs that documented agriculture, livelihoods, waterscapes, and landscapes. He began focusing on the Arizona-Sonoran Desert area, specifically the area now designated as Saguaro National Park, intensively in 1931 and continued for about three decades. Unfortunately, many of the people in his images are not identified. William Adolphus "Dolph" Evans is using a large format camera to document the park's plant life (Courtesy University of Arizona Creative Center for Photography.)

Homer Shantz took this photograph of Dolph Evans (right) and Mr. Matheson in April 1930. The only concession to informality was they both removed their coats. They are sitting on a ghost saguaro, which is a cactus that has lived more than 100 years and has deteriorated to a skeleton of ribs. Neckties, vests, and long-sleeved white shirts are still very much the fashion of the day. (Courtesy University of Arizona Creative Center for Photography.)

The University of Arizona grounds were planted extensively by Homer Shantz and his students, who collected botanical specimens, brought them back, and planted them in the grounds. Many of the desert plants came from the Saguaro National Park. In 2002, the University of Arizona grounds were included in the National Register of Historic Places as a Historical Botanical Garden. (Courtesy University of Arizona Creative Center for Photography.)

Mr. Bridge(s) evidently had a strong interest in botany when he visited the Saguaro National Park in 1931. When Shantz took this photograph, the area had not yet been designated as Saguaro National Monument. (Courtesy University of Arizona Creative Center for Photography.)

Shantz never missed an opportunity to show off the newly created Saguaro National Monument, as in this 1935 photograph of the Phoenix Garden Club. They made the 120-mile trip to Tucson and then ate their lunch while Dr. Shantz presented his lecture. Afterward, they were free to explore the area. Of course, no woman would dream of attending a meeting without wearing a hat. (Courtesy University of Arizona Creative Center for Photography.)

For many years, the Horseless Carriage Club of America made annual excursions through Saguaro National Park. They could hike, picnic, attempt to figure out where they were, or make whatever repairs were necessary on their vehicles. This vehicle is a Model T of 1913 vintage. (Courtesy Saguaro National Park.)

John C. Phillips came to Phoenix in 1898 to establish a law practice, but he could not make a living at his profession, so he hired himself to help with the construction of the new state capitol building, which he would occupy as governor from 1929 to 1931. John Calhoun Phillips, born November 13, 1870, in Illinois, studied law at Hedding College and was admitted to the Illinois Bar in 1896. An avid hunter and fisherman, he worked for Arizona conservation laws and led the establishment of the Arizona Game and Fish Department. He loved horseback riding in Saguaro National Park. Phillips died on June 25, 1943. (Courtesy Saguaro National Park.)

In 1884, twenty-year-old Levi Howell Manning arrived in Tucson and began his career as a reporter for the *Arizona Daily Star* and the *Tucson Citizen* newspapers. During his career, Manning would rise to the positions of general manager of the Ice and Electric Company, surveyor-general for the Arizona Territory (appointed by President Cleveland), and mayor of Tucson from 1905 to 1907. Manning also was a major force in bringing the electric trolley to the area, but his primary interest was in ranching; he built an elegant summer cabin on land that is now part of the Saguaro National Park. (Courtesy Saguaro National Park.)

A wonderful creek ran by the Manning Cabin, providing an escape from Tucson's summer heat. In 1904, Manning filed for a 160-acre homestead in the Rincon Mountains where he planned to build a summer cabin. Mexican workmen constructed an 11-mile wagon road to the proposed cabin site. The following year, Manning erected tents on his land in which to house a Mexican workforce while they built his cabin. Provisions, tools, and equipment were taken to the area by packhorse and wagon. Manning's ranch foreman, David Waldon, oversaw construction of the cabin. Trees for the cabin were felled in the immediate area. Manning was the first to build such a cabin retreat in the mountains. (Courtesy Saguaro National Park.)

Manning's cabin was a log structure, and daubing sealed the cracks between the logs. Rolled roofing covered the sheathing that was placed over the log trusses. The interior of the cabin consisted of a living room with a fireplace, a kitchen, two bedrooms, and two small bunk rooms. Manning had grand plans for entertaining in his summer cabin, and he had a piano hauled by wagon to the cabin. (Courtesy Saguaro National Park.)

In 1907, Manning's homestead rights were revoked, and that area of the Rincon Mountains was attached to the Santa Catalina Division of the Coronado National Forest. By 1968, the park was using the cabin as its firefighting headquarters. The man wearing glasses in the foreground is Thomas Carroll. (Courtesy Saguaro National Park.)

Unfortunately, the names of these people have been lost to the mists of history. This photograph was taken on the exterior of the east side of the cabin at the juncture of the living room and the central area. The vertical daubed slabs enclosed a bedroom. In 1922, the forest service moved its firefighting quarters for its fire watch and trail crew from Spud Rock Cabin to Manning's cabin. (Courtesy Saguaro National Park.)

When the forest service took over the cabin in 1922, the structure was reroofed and a concrete floor was poured. Three men stayed there. Two kept the fire trails serviceable, and one man, pictured here, rode horseback on a fireguard patrol, making two rounds per day on a circuit of four lookout points. (Courtesy Saguaro National Park.)

The vegetation at the higher elevation of the Manning Cabin is quite different from the lower saguaro and cacti of the desert. (Courtesy Saguaro National Park.)

Everyone pitched in on laundry day at the Manning Camp. The washing machine may seem primitive, but in 1905, it cost $5.62. Around 1905, the electric washing machine was invented, but electricity did not reach Saguaro National Park until December 1941. Clothes had to be rinsed and wrung out by hand. The dryer was the cool outdoor breeze. (Courtesy Saguaro National Park.)

The picture of this woman, who appears dressed to go horseback riding, was taken outside of the Manning Cabin around 1906. The riding habit would have been for riding sidesaddle, and it was similar to the clothing she would have worn in everyday life. It was not specifically designed for sidesaddle riding, but sidesaddle habit design still tended to follow fashion of the day. This safety skirt, introduced in 1875, later evolved into the open-sided apron. (Courtesy Saguaro National Park.)

This image was also taken between 1906 and 1907. This well-dressed woman is not wearing a sidesaddle habit, but with those boots, she is certainly ready to ride at a moment's notice. (Courtesy Saguaro National Park.)

Levi Manning had an 11-mile road constructed from Tucson to the cabin so that wagons, such as the one seen in this image, could bring in supplies for the cabin. (Courtesy Saguaro National Park.)

Levi's son Howell was able to supply the park service with details on the Manning Cabin recalled from the years 1906 and 1907, which he spent at the cabin. Howell had attended Culver Military Academy and Dartmouth College before joining the Army as a machine gunner during World War I. His life fell apart when, just before Christmas in 1951, a drunk driver crashed into a car his son, Howell Jr., was driving from Tucson to his Canoa ranch. Howell Jr. and two companions were killed instantly. Despondent and lacking a male heir interested in ranching, Howell Sr. started selling off the family homestead. He died in 1967. Pictured here is Howard Manning, son of Howell Jr., at the Manning cabin. (Courtesy WACC.)

Frank Stansberry is shown pulling the latest in fence wire stringing machines in 1957. Note that the wire coil is ahead of the wheels. The more wire that is uncoiled, the more increase there is on the back pull of the cart. (Courtesy WACC.)

Two of the park's firefighters, Frank Duffield (left) and Bob Vanover, stand outside the Manning Cabin in 1943. At this time, the cabin served as the park's firefighting headquarters. (Courtesy WACC.)

Trail laborer Charles F. Drewes is pictured here with a National Park Service mule named Kate. The Desert Ecology Trail (a quarter-mile round trip on the paved trail) is an easy track along the Cactus Forest Drive. Signs along the way introduce the plants and animals that call Saguaro National Park home. This trail is wheelchair accessible. (Courtesy WACC.)

In 1968, future Saguaro National Park superintendent William F. Paleck (left) worked as a fire control aid. His two friends are John C. Everhart (center), also a fire control aid, and Jon W. Erickson (right). In 1971, Saguaro National Monument developed its first Fire Management Plan. (Courtesy WACC.)

In 1960, these three ladies were listed as "notable visitors" to Saguaro National Park. From left to right, they are Mrs. Tom Allen, Mrs. Arno Demaray, and Mrs. Hugh Miller. They were the wives of National Park Service regional director Tim Allen, assistant regional director Arthur Demaray, and Hugh Miller of Saguaro National Park. (Courtesy WACC.)

By the 1960s, well-dressed visitors were flocking to the park. In this photograph, a park ranger has just finished giving an interpretive talk. (Courtesy WACC.)

Getting Dr. James Mielke to the top of saguaro is not easy task. In 1941, scientists worried about the decline of the saguaro population. That year, Paul Lightle, Lake Gill, and James Mielke counted all 13,304 cacti in Saguaro National Park Rincon Mountain District, Section no. 17. (Courtesy WACC.)

In the spring of 1945, engineer Dr. James Mielke of the Bureau of Plant Industry, Soils, and Agriculture checks on the healing of an amputated branch of a saguaro from the previous season. After monitoring the plots for nine years, it was determined that there was no evidence to support the opinion that a contagious bacterial disease and continued lack of saguaro reproduction in the cactus forest was a major problem. (Courtesy WACC.)

Examining a saguaro for bacterial disease is a prickly job. The symptoms may appear at one or more positions on the trunk or branches of saguaros. The bacterial infestation of saguaros would prove to be just another part of a desert ecosystem. (Courtesy Arizona Historical Society.)

Dr. Alice Boyle of the Plant Pathology Department at the University of Arizona is treating the bacteria by thoroughly washing the diseased pocket with 10-percent household bleach solution (one part Clorox, nine parts of water, and one teaspoon of liquid detergent per gallon of solution) and then allow the pocket to stand open to hasten healing. (Courtesy Arizona Historical Society.)

No one is quite certain just when visitors started making pleasure trips to the Saguaro National Park area, but these people of all ages are certainly from the late 1800s. One would be at a loss to figure out how to keep these lovely light dresses looking so fresh in the dusty desert. (Courtesy Arizona Historical Society.)

From the lookout, visitors enjoy a 360-degree view of the area and can spot many important landmarks. (Courtesy National Park Service Denver.)

Jean Arthur was at the height of her prestige on the Columbia lot when the movie *Arizona* went into production at Old Tucson Studio on the edge of Saguaro National Park West. There are many scenes of saguaros throughout the movie. In this 1940 film, Arthur plays Phoebe Titus—hard riding yet beautiful in a gown—and was perfect for the part. It was decided to shoot the film in black and white because of the threat of war and Arizona was just then emerging from the Great Depression. Columbia wanted Gary Cooper for the male lead but settled for the cheaper Joel McCrea; however, William Holden eventually replaced Joel McCrea. Holden was only 22—thirteen years younger than Arthur when the film was shot. (Courtesy Old Tucson Movie Studios.)

As Saguaro National Park developed, more and more attention was given to educating and entertaining the park visitors. (Courtesy National Park Service Denver.)

Areas with clusters of desert plants and an identification box provided visitors with easy access to information. (Courtesy National Park Service Denver.)

In the 1950s, visitors could purchase a booklet describing the area plants for 15¢. (Courtesy National Park Service Denver.)

A hike in Saguaro National Park East or West can be a leisurely stroll on a short trail or a long strenuous trek; however, both districts also offer driving tours. The interpretive signs leave little doubt as to where the visitor is and what he or she will see. The Rincon Mountains rise to higher than 8,000 feet in Saguaro National Park East. (Courtesy National Park Service Denver.)

The Cactus Forest Drive is a one-way paved road that runs through the heart of the saguaro forest in the Saguaro National Park East and offers a leisurely look at a wide variety of Sonoran Desert life. (Courtesy National Park Service Denver.)

A drive through the cactus forest is a wonderful way to enjoy the Saguaro forest. However, there are sharp turns, so it is best to take it slow. (Courtesy National Park Service Denver.)

The Ez-Kim-In-Zin picnic area in Saguaro National Park West, a remote, beautiful site, honors the Aravaipa Apache chief Ezkiminzin, who lost all of his family in the Fort Grant Massacre. On the afternoon of April 28, 1871, six Tucsonans, 48 Mexicans, and 92 Tohono O'odham rode to Aravaipa Canyon. Two days later, they surrounded the Aravaipa Apache camp while most of the men were off hunting. The raiders killed almost everyone in the camp. Out of 144 dead, all but eight were women and children. Many children were sold into slavery in Mexico. (Author's collection.)

Safford Peak, known locally as "Sombrero Peak" because of its shape, was named for the third Arizona territorial governor, Anson P.K. Safford, in 1869. Safford turned down a nomination for the US House of Representatives before being appointed to the office of Arizona surveyor-general by Pres. Andrew Johnson. He was nominated for Arizona territorial governor by Pres. Ulysses S. Grant. Safford believed in the public school system and established schools throughout the Arizona Territory. Safford Peak, located in Saguaro National Park West, is covered with the saguaros. (Author's collection.)

The saguaro, the monarch of the desert, is an icon of the Southwest. It is renowned for the variety of its strange shapes, which inspire wonderful imaginings. The arrangement of the arms or branches gives each saguaro a distinctive personality. (Courtesy University of Arizona Creative Center for Photography.)

To fully appreciate the saguaro, take a walk through the valley of the giants. At the end of its first year, the saguaro may measure only a quarter of an inch. At 30 years, the saguaro may flower and produce fruits. After 75 years, it may sprout its first branches. By 150 years, the saguaro may be as tall as 50 feet and weigh eight tons. The saguaro's huge mass is supported by a cylindrical framework of long woody ribs. (Courtesy University of Arizona Creative Center for Photography.)

Young saguaros and seedlings grow under sheltering plants known as nurse trees. They are protected from the intense sunlight; covered from winter cold; and hidden from rodents, birds, and other animals. Rocks may also provide protection for the young saguaros. Nurse trees are generally palo verde, ironwood, or mesquite. Often the nurse tree dies when the saguaro reaches maturity. Competition by the saguaro may take water and soil nutrients from the nurse tree. (Author's collection.)

Saguaro cacti sometimes grow in odd or misshapen forms. The growing tip occasionally produces a fan-like form that is crested, or cristate. Even though crested saguaros are somewhat rare, more than 25 have been found within the park boundaries. Biologists disagree as to the cause of this unusual form. Some speculate that it is a genetic mutation, while others believe the form is the result of a lightning strike or freeze damage. (Courtesy US Fish and Wildlife Service.)

Dr. Homer Shantz captured this magnificent view of the saguaro forest in 1935. (Courtesy Center for Creative Photograph)

BIBLIOGRAPHY

Ayer, E.H. *Arizona Wildflowers: A Guide to Common Species*. Frederick, CO: Renaissance House, 1989.

Benson, L. *The Cacti of the United States and Canada*. Stanford: Stanford University Press, 1982.

Desert Botanical Garden. *Wildflowers: A Guide to Identifying, Locating, and Enjoying Arizona Wildflowers and Cactus Blossoms*. Phoenix: Arizona Highways, 1988.

Earle, W.H. *Cacti of the Southwest*. Tempe: Rancho Arroyo Book Distributor, 1980.

Fontana, Bernard and John P. Schaefer. *Of Earth and Little Rain*. Flagstaff: Northland Press, 1981.

Hodge, C. *All About Saguaros*. Phoenix: Arizona Highways, 1991.

Nabhan, G.P. *Gathering the Desert*. Tucson: University of Arizona Press, 1985.

Nelson, R. and S. *Field Guide to Common Desert Cactus of Arizona*. Phoenix: Primer Publishers, 1996.

Steenbergh, W.F. and C.H. Lowe. *Ecology of the Saguaro: II. Reproduction, Germination, Establishment, Growth, and Survival of the Young Plant*. National Park Service Scientific Monograph Series No. 8, 1977.

Turner, R.M., J.E. Bowers, and T.L. Burgess. *Sonoran Desert Plants: An Ecological Atlas*. Tucson: University of Arizona Press, 1995.

INDEX

Arnberger, Robert, 82
Burns, Hal, 27
Cammerer, Arno, 16
Carrillo, Emilio, 46
Clinton, William Jefferson, 9, 30
Converse, James, 7, 8, 53, 55
Cote, Robert, 57
Craighead, Sarah, 87
Demaray, Arno E., 16
Egermayer, Don, 66
Egermayer, Ruth, 66, 67
Evans, William Adolphus, 94, 95
Freeman family, 49–51
Giles, Robert L., 80
Greenway, Isabella, 9, 14
Hayden, Carl Trumbull, 9
Hoover, Herbert, 7, 9, 10
Ickes, Harold L., 7, 12, 14
Jelks, Rukin, 52
Jones, Harold, 81

Judge, Paul A., 80
Kennedy, John F., 9, 30
Lindbergh, Charles, 27
Manning, Howell, 107
Manning, Levi Howell, 100–102
Manning, Reg, 29
Morris, Douglas, 83
Oury, William S., 48
Paleck, William, 84, 85, 100
Pinkley, Frank, 8, 9, 17
Roosevelt, Franklin Delano, 7, 9, 11
Shantz, Homer, 8–10, 93
Sidles, Darla, 23, 88
Tillotson, H.R., 9, 74
Udall, Morris, 9, 15
Udall, Stewart, 8, 9, 15
Van Alstine family, 62
Walker, Franklin, 86
Winn, Fred, 17

Discover Thousands of Local History Books Featuring Millions of Vintage Images

Arcadia Publishing, the leading local history publisher in the United States, is committed to making history accessible and meaningful through publishing books that celebrate and preserve the heritage of America's people and places.

Find more books like this at
www.arcadiapublishing.com

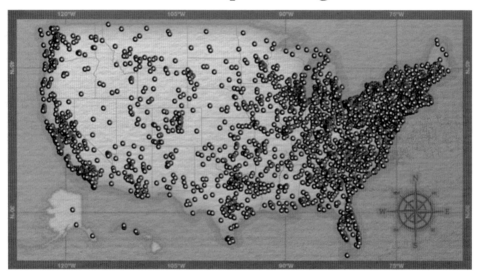

Search for your hometown history, your old stomping grounds, and even your favorite sports team.